**THE ARTS
SOCIETY**
EAST SURREY
AREA

CONTENTS

**THE ARTS
SOCIETY
EAST SURREY
AREA**

INTRODUCTION

This is one of several "50 Treasures" books produced by Arts Society Areas around the UK.

This book covers The Arts Society East Surrey Area which is possibly the smallest geographical Arts Society Area within the UK – about 20 miles from Chipstead to East Horsley and about 24 miles from Limpsfield to West Horsley., although there are 15 member societies within that area.

So, we thought it might be difficult to find 50 treasures within this small area. After all we don't have the possible range that is available to very much larger areas such as the North West or South West of the UK. But not so! There is a wide range of fascinating and not always well-known places, objects and buildings within East Surrey and we have chosen 50 which we think are interesting. Several possibilities have been left out, mainly for reasons of similarity or because there are too many within the same small area (for instance the Holbein Hall at Reigate, the animal enclosures at Nutfield, Betchworth and Dorking, Titsey Place, East Horsley Towers, The Thorndike Theatre and others). But we think the range and interest shows just how varied and rich in history and art a small geographical area can be!

We hope that you enjoy getting to know more about the treasures of the Surrey Hills within East Surrey.

Michael Beach and Paul Fletcher

**THE ARTS
SOCIETY**
EAST SURREY
AREA

FOREWORD
ANDREA GABB, AREA CHAIRMAN,
THE ARTS SOCIETY, EAST SURREY AREA

This must be the most appropriate year of all years, to publish a book about our local countryside and its treasures.

All of us, whether we live on top of a hill with no buildings in view, or like me, in a street with houses on either side, have access to the most amazing walks, views, cycle rides and drives within easy reach.

And this year we have been so grateful for that. So glad that, when the weather has been kind, we've been able to get out and explore our local area of East Surrey. Walking has been a saviour for many. We've been closer to the seasons, closer to our wooded hills and secret valleys, and to the natural world that inhabits them.

So what more appropriate than, as the world starts to regains some normality, we have a book of our own to celebrate the places we have, the history we have, and the quirky secret buildings and monuments that have been hidden in our midst.

However far you have walked in the last twelve months, I guarantee that none of you will know every single Treasure in this book. So explore some more, enjoy what we have and let's all be grateful for where we live.

My great thanks to those who've worked hard on this book to pull it together, particularly Michael Beach and Paul Fletcher, who've done the researching, the writing and many of the photographs.

And our thanks also to Dave Barham, who's made a wonderful job of the printing, as always.

March 2021

Lumley Chapel Cheam

The Chapel, which stands in the grounds of the parish church of St Dunstan's, is the only surviving remnant of the original medieval parish church- a 900-year-old building that stood on this site and is the chancel of that original building.

In the 1500s Lord John Lumley established it as a memorial for himself and his two wives. Lord Lumley was a connoisseur of books and on his death his large library was purchased by King James I and became the basis of the Royal Library and later the British Library.

The Chapel contains a number of interesting memorials including alabaster and marble monuments to his two wives. Plus, a beautiful plaster decorated ceiling and some fine brasses.

The chapel is the oldest building in Cheam and is a part of a village green which includes some beautiful old cottages and The Whitehall a timber framed 15th century house which is now a local arts centre.

Further Information

St Dunstan's Church, Church Farm Lane, Cheam SM3 8QH.

The chapel is in the care of the Church Conservation Trust and is open daily – the key is available at the library opposite.

Images: Thomas Leitch

Leatherhead Institute Sculpture

The Letherhead Institute (original town spelling) was given to the community by Abraham Dixon in 1892 for social, leisure and educational purposes, a function that it still fulfills today.

In 2012 the building had a new attraction added to its Victorian façade with the addition of a metal sculpture to mark the Diamond Jubilee of Queen Elizabeth II, the Olympic Road Races (which passed through the area) and 120 years of the Institute.

The sculpture was created by the young people of the Leatherhead Youth Project in conjunction with the Fire and Iron Gallery, an arts centre that specializes in metal and runs special exhibitions and permanent displays of everything from jewellery to sculpture.

Further Information

The sculpture can be seen from the street on the façade of the building
Leatherhead Institute 67 High Street, Leatherhead KT22 8AH.

The Fire and Iron Gallery is open at usual opening times
Rowhurst, Oxshott Road, Leatherhead, KT22 0EN.

Images: June Robinson

The Saxon Church Albury

The church dates from just before the Norman conquest and was the village church until the village was moved down the road in the 18th century, to extend the parkland. It now stands alone in private parkland. Facing you as you enter the church is a splendid 15th century wall painting of St Christopher.

There is a Roman base to the font (the bowl is in the village church) a 13th century piscina, and a tablet commemorating William Oughtred, whose book Clavis Mathematicae is the origin of the multiplication 'x'.

But the major interest is the Drummond Chapel. Sir Henry Drummond had the 13th century transept re-designed as his family mausoleum and chose Augustus Pugin to do it. Pugin designed the windows, the walls, roof, altar, floor and memorials. It is rich in colour and a spectacular example of his work. Here is Pugin at his best: a real contrast to the simplicity of the 15th century wall painting – two wonderful pieces of decorative art separated by centuries.

Further Information

St Peter and St Paul, Albury Park, Albury GU5 9BB.

The church is open every day from 9am and is in Albury Park which is private land but the owners have given permission to park for viewing the church.

Image: Michael Beach

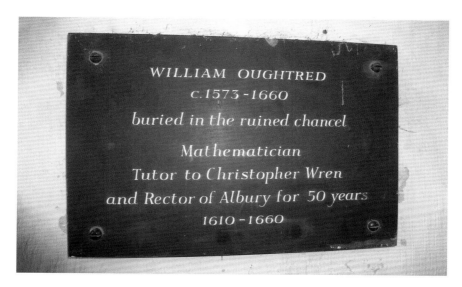

WILLIAM OUGHTRED
c.1573 -1660

buried in the ruined chancel

Mathematician
Tutor to Christopher Wren
and Rector of Albury for 50 years
1610 -1660

Coal Tax Posts

From late medieval times until 1891, the Corporation of London had the right to levy taxes on coal brought into the city. Originally, the coal was transported by sea and up the Thames to the Port of London, but, with the coming of better roads, canals and railways, collection of the duty became more complicated. In 1861 the London Coal and Wine Duties Continuance Act defined the area for collection of duties to correspond with that of the Metropolitan Police District established in 1839. This followed parish boundaries and the area was demarcated by 280 coal posts of which about 210 remain.

The posts were of four basic types, the most common being type 2 (with slight variations), as illustrated. These were made in cast iron by Henry Grissell at the Regents Canal Ironworks and most bear the shield from the City of London arms and an inscription referring to the Act of Parliament under which they were set up.

Further Information

The coal post illustrated is no. 141 on Walton Heath 100 yards along a footpath leading southeast from the Dorking Road (B2032) to the north of the junction with Deans Lane. No. 140 is at the start of the footpath. The ironworks plaque is from post no. 142, 150 yards further along the footpath. For a complete list of the coal tax posts and their positions around London see: www.rhaworth.net

Images: Marion Woodward

A Quartet of Drama

We are lucky to have within the area a rich source of drama provided by four major amateur "little theatres" which present, between them, some thirty to forty different productions a year covering the classics, musicals and comedy. Real dramatic treasures!

The Archway in Horley is based under a range of railway arches beneath Horley Station and produces ten plays a year each running for ten nights in addition to a wide range of studio productions.

The Miller Centre in Caterham is housed in a community-based building that by day is a leisure centre and by night a theatre! Nine productions are presented in a year each one running for ten performances (including a Saturday matinee).

The Courtyard in Chipstead is the home of the Chipstead Players, a purpose-built theatre originally a stable. Six or seven productions are presented annually each for five performances.

Nomads in Horsley have a purpose-built theatre, The Nomad Theatre, which presents around twelve productions a year for four or five nights.

Further Information

www.archwaytheatre.com
www.millercentretheatre.org
www.chipsteadplayers.org
www.nomadtheatre.com

Bourne Hall Ewell

Bourne Hall is a museum, library, café and meeting place set in the grounds of the former Bourne Hall, which includes the pools of the Hogmill river. The pools were popular with pre-Raphaelite painters including Holman Hunt and John Millais who painted his Death of Ophelia there.

The original Hall was replaced in the 1970s by a spectacular space-age circular building. This Grade II listed building was designed by Alwyn Sheppard Fidler who was previously chief architect of Crawley New Town. The fascinating museum has a wide range of exhibits from pre-historic times to the modern age and includes Lord Rosebery's hansom cab, and a 19th century fire engine along with fine art, social history and Roman remains from local sites.

Further Information

Bourne Hall Spring Street, Ewell KT17 1UF.

The museum is free and is open along with the café and library during regular opening hours.

www.bournehall.org

Images: Thomas Leitch

St Nicolas and Jane Austen

St Nicolas in Great Bookham has been the site of a church since the 7th century and the remains of Saxon wall paintings can still be seen. The church has some fine stained glass windows and a number of notable memorials, all of which are well worth visiting. But probably the major interest of the church is that the Rev. Samuel Cooke was the vicar of Great Bookham from 1769-1820 and he was godfather to Jane Austen and husband of Mrs Austen's cousin.

How often Jane Austen visited is not known but she is said to have spent time in Bookham whilst writing several of her novels and its location is consistent with place details in 'Emma' and her unfinished novel 'The Watsons' features Dorking in its narrative.

There are also other well-known names associated with Great Bookham. Fanny Burney lived in the village and C.S Lewis studied privately in Bookham in 1917 while Pink Floyd singer Roger Waters was born in Great Bookham in 1943!

Further Information

St Nicolas, Lower Road, Great Bookham, KT23 3PN.

The church is usually open daily.

www.stnicolasbookham.org.uk

Images: top - Michael Beach, bottom - Wikimedia Commons

St Margaret's Church, Chipstead

There has been worship at St Margaret's Church, Chipstead, for 800 years and probably a site of worship for much longer. The ancient yew tree that blew down in the storm of 1987 traditionally marked a place of pre-Christian worship. It had been dated as being 1,200 years old.

Inside the church are many interesting features ancient and modern, including the stone font dating from the 14th century, with a beautiful cover carved by a parishioner from the fallen yew tree. There is an inscription over the entrance of the more recent porch – 'Templa quam delecta': How lovely is your dwelling place. (Psalm 84 verse 1.)

In the listed churchyard (still in use) is a recently formed Prayer Walk, seven stones carved with the 'I am' sayings of Jesus (the first being just inside the lychgate – 'I am the gate.')

Further Information

Church Lane Chipstead CR5 3RD.

The church may be approached from the west via Elmore Road which turns off High Road by Elmore Pond or from the east up Star Lane from the A23 Brighton Road.

The church is usually locked when not in use but the churchyard is open to all.

www.stmargaretschipstead.org

Images: Marion Woodward, Kim Honey

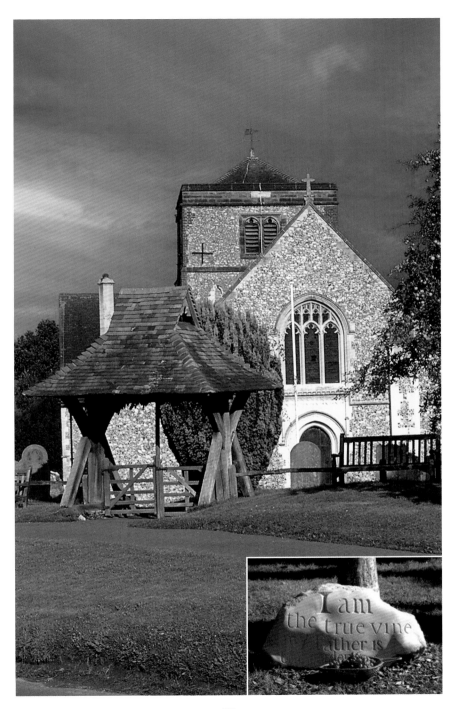

Ashtead Pottery

Ashtead had its own pottery although it did not source its clay locally. The Victoria Works pottery was set up in 1923 with the aim of providing work for disabled ex-servicemen. Starting with just four workers, they eventually employed forty men who were recruited from all over southern England.

The driving force in starting the factory was Sir Lawrence Weaver who had a great deal of help from Clough Williams-Ellis (creator of Portmeirion village) and Stafford Cripps, a prominent politician of the time. As the workforce grew, Purcell Close, Ashtead was built to accommodate men with families. The output of the pottery was extremely varied. There were figurines, commemoratives, ornamental wares and crockery in bold bright colours. Leading artists of the day designed for the pottery. One of these was Phoebe Stabler who also designed for both Royal Doulton and Poole Pottery. The pottery closed in 1935 but its wares are very collectable. They include such items as the Christopher Robin Nursery Ware and souvenirs of the 1924 Wembley Exhibition.

Look out for Ashtead Pottery in antique shops and centres and car boot sales.

Further Information

Examples of the whole range of the pottery can be seen on the website
www.ashtead pottery.com

Image: reproduced by permission

Bletchingley – Clayton monument

Sir Robert Clayton was a prominent entrepreneur, politician and philanthropist of the Stuart era. He lived at Marden Park near Woldingham and did three stints as one of two MPs in the erstwhile 'rotten borough' of Bletchingley where his memorial resides in St Mary's Church. It is the only surviving signed work by the sculptor Richard Crutcher and represents Sir Robert and his wife beneath a substantial aedicule – a sort of panel enclosed by columns with a pediment above. The marble monument dates from 1705, two years before Sir Robert's death and is considered to be one of the finest examples of 18th Century work in the country.

In the 1960s Archbishop Desmond Tutu was a curate at Bletchingley. His image close by the monument is a reminder of those rather different times.

Further Information

Church Walk, Bletchingley RH1 4PD.

www.bletchingleyparishchurch.org.uk

Image: Paul Fletcher

Westhumble Station

Appearing in the "100 Best Stations" by Simon Jenkins is Westhumble Station. A Grade II listed building, it was opened in 1867 and built at the insistence of Thomas Grissell, the then owner of Norbury Park, in compensation for the railway cutting across his land.

Designed in the Châteauesque style by Charles Driver, it includes pitched roofs, an ornamental turret and patterned tiles. Still in use as a station, it is a gateway to Box Hill and surrounding countryside and will be familiar to anyone who watches the beginning of each episode of 'Great British Railway Journeys'.

Within a few moments' walk of the station there are a number of interesting features. Opposite is the house where the renowned organist Lady Susie Jeans lived and taught until her death in 1993 while a little further up the road is where the Victorian novelist Fanny Burney lived and opposite that is the Chapel of Ease, built in the early 1800s with interesting architecture, attractive interior and charming garden.

Further Information

Westhumble Street, Westhumble RH5 6BT.

The station is just off the A24 between Dorking and Box Hill.

All of the buildings are easily viewed and are only a few minutes' walk from the station along Westhumble Street.

Image: Thomas Leitch

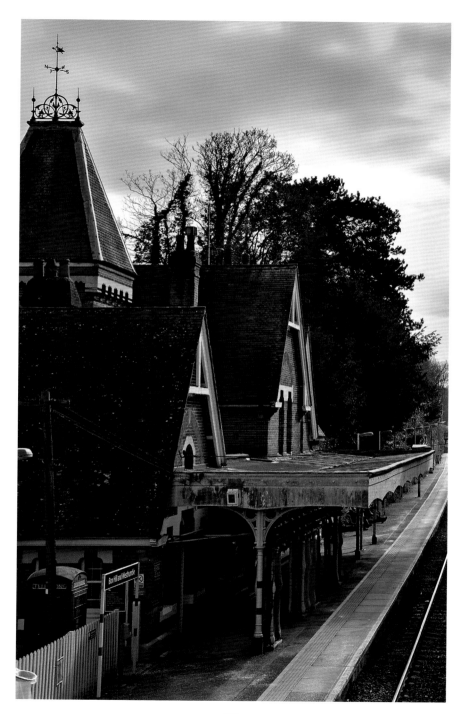

All Saints' Church, Banstead

The glowing colours and humane draughtsmanship of windows designed in stained and painted glass by the firm of Clayton & Bell are immediately striking.

A particular favourite is the Epiphany window on the North side, installed about 1880 in memory of Henry Lambert. Its three lights depict the Magi bringing gifts to the Christ-child: on the left a young page holds the bridle of a disdainful camel, while his master walks ahead over the cobbled path with his jar of myrrh; in the centre one stands clutching a golden cylinder, and one has fallen to his knees, his incense jar trailing its chain. Behind them a shooting star blazes through the sky. The third light shows the Holy Family, the Child holding his arms wide and welcoming. Above them all three angels hold scrolls quoting (in Latin) St Luke's Gospel, and at the base is a quotation from the prophet Isaiah.

Detailed cartoons survive for this window, a rare find, and are now in the Surrey History Centre.

Further Information

All Saints' Church, High Street, Banstead SM7 2NG.

All Saints' Church is on the south side of Banstead High Street, set back behind a green space.

Normally the church is open on weekdays from about 9.00am to 4.45pm.
www.bansteadallsaints.com

Images: Alan Clarke

Outwood Windmill

The Windmill on Outwood Common is a Grade 1 listed building and is regarded as the oldest working windmill in Britain. It was built for Thomas Budgen, a miller from Nutfield, in 1665 before the Fire of London. Tradition has it that the builders watched the fire 25 miles away. The original deeds are still in existence. Thomas Budgen was convicted as a seditious preacher in 1678 and fined £20!

Over many years it has received considerable renovations including, of course, new sails.

The mill is easily seen as it dominates Outwood Common. It is in private hands, although in the past it has produced and sold flour and been opened for visits.

Further Information

Outwood Windmill, Outwood Common, Redhill RH1 5PW.

Image: Outwood Windmill

St. Agatha's Church, Woldingham

St. Agatha's is situated on the edge of the village about three quarters of a mile to the south of St. Paul's (which replaced it as Woldingham's parish church in 1934.) There has been a church on the site for many hundreds of years and the present one is believed to be the smallest church in Surrey. By 1832 the original church had become very dilapidated and a Mr Jones of Upper Court Manor had a replacement built. This building was restored in 1889 by Sir Walpole Greenwell of Marden Park. It is built of flint and comprises a single room approximately 30ft by 20ft which seats at most 40 people. There is a small porch with mock timber framing. The roof is pitched and covered with plain clay tiles. The west end gable is extended to form a bell turret built of sandstone that is surmounted by a weather vane. There is a single bell, which was rehung in 2017. A cross standing on the east gable disappeared at some time in the past, and in 2018 was replaced by a new one, whose design is based on old drawings and photographs.

The church is currently open for private prayer on Sundays and Wednesdays and is a place of peace and tranquillity for those visiting the original churchyard, where Woldingham residents have been buried for several hundred years

Further Information

Church Road Woldingham CR3 7JG.

Contact the Revd. Dr. Catherine Dowland-Pillinger on 01883 652192.

Image: Peter Johnson

Banstead Woods

The Woods are 230 acres of ancient woodland and the area is designated as a Local Nature Reserve and SSSI. There are wonderful dog walks through different habitats and a refreshing pond for four-footed friends. Until the late 15th century the Woods were enclosed as a deer park for the use of the Kings of England and, until Catherine of Aragon, were given to the Queen as a gift on ascending the throne. For the last 500 years, ownership has passed from Lords of the Manor until now when it is maintained by Reigate & Banstead Borough Council and Surrey County Council. There are many interesting features such as the deer park boundary; an old orchard that was part of the King's hunting lodge and the foundations of the WW2 prisoner of war huts that were home to Italian and German internees.

Walking groups and running clubs use the wide and generally well-maintained paths and in 2017 a Narnia trail was installed with wonderful carvings from standing deadwood of characters from C S Lewis's books to captivate the youngsters.

Further Information

Holly Lane, Banstead CR5 3NR.

Holly Lane runs south from the western end of Banstead High Street. Banstead Woods car park is on the right just before the junction with Outwood Lane.

Free car park.

Image: Marion Woodward

The Durdans Stables Gate

The Durdans was already a well-established racing stables when Lord Rosebery purchased them in 1872. There are several Grade II* listed buildings at The Durdans as well as the listed horse graves and gates.

Near to the main entrance to The Durdans on Chalk Lane, Epsom are the beautiful Grade II listed iron gates which were built in the early 1700s for the Duke of Chandos' Palace known as Canons and they bear the Chandos motto. It is thought they could have been made by a pupil of Jean Tijou who produced the gates for Hampton Court. When the palace was demolished in 1747 the gates were brought to The Durdans.

Lord Rosebery loved The Durdans and spent much of his time there as horses and racing were his passion, resulting in three Derby winners. During the First World War Lord Rosebery is said to have locked the gates on bidding farewell to his son, Neil, stating that he would only open them again when his son returned. Sadly, his son was killed in Palestine in 1917 and so never returned. The gates have never been opened since except during conservation work in 2013.

Further Information

Chalk Lane Epsom KT18 7AX.

Chalk Lane is a narrow road at the corner of Langley Vale Road and the B290 Ashley Road, Epsom. It is best to park somewhere on Epsom Downs and walk down.

The gates are always visible as are a view of the grounds and house.

Image: Michael Beach

Buckland Windmill

Buckland Windmill is in the garden of 'Yewdells', a Grade II listed house built in 1713 for John Udall—from which the house name is derived. John Udall was the Buckland Estate carpenter. Three generations of Udalls managed the business before it passed to the Sanders family around 1840. From 1840 through to the 1950s, five generations of the Sanders family ran a sawyer's business from the site and the windmill is the power for the saw.

The windmill, also Grade II listed, was built in the 1860-1870 period. This build date is confirmed by the plaque detailing 'W Cooper of Henfield' who operated as a millwright from 1854-1876.

The windmill was rediscovered and restored by the new owners of Yewdells from 1994 to 2002. It is the only surviving wind-powered sawmill remaining in the UK.

Further Information

Yewdells, Dungates Lane, Buckland RH3 7BD.

The windmill is in the garden of Yewdells and can be seen from the Lane. Pre-book appointment to visit with Duncan Ferns, 07786 966841.

Image: Duncan Ferns

Hatchments

Many Surrey churches display lozenge-shaped funerary hatchments. 'Hatchment' is a corrupted version of 'achievements'. Dating from the 15th century it was the custom when landed gentry died to hang their hatchment above the door of their house during the period of mourning and then display it in the church where they worshipped. The heraldic images in the hatchment represent that person's achievements.

One of Mickleham church's six hatchments is that of Sir Lucas Pepys of Juniper Hill who died in 1830. He was a physician to George III. The coronet at the top is that of a baronet. The shield indicates he was a man (a woman's would be lozenged shaped). This is divided in half with his wife's coat of arms on the right. The escutcheon with the hand indicates that his first wife was an heiress. The white background on the right shows that his second wife is still alive. Many hatchments have the legend *RESURGAM* meaning 'I will rise again'. Sir Lucas' has the Pepys family motto *MENS CUIUSQUE IS EST QUISQUE* 'The mind's the man' from Cicero's De Re Publica.

Further Information

St Michael and All Angels, Old London Road, Mickleham RH5 6DU.

Image: Ben Tatham

The Old Well, Banstead

The Old Well stands on a triangular grassed island at the junction of Park Road and Woodmansterne Lane and was originally the centre of the village. It is almost 300 feet deep and was the public source of water for the village until about 1895 when a mains supply became available.

The wellhead structure is Grade II listed and dates from the 18th century. The elaborate winding gear and wooden well cover survive within, accessed via a gate on the western side. The building was restored in 2003. Two important houses in Woodmansterne Lane took their names from their proximity to the Well. Well House on the north side (now the site of Well House flats) was the home of Sir Daniel Lambert, Lord Mayor of London in 1741, and Well Farm on the south side is the oldest house in Banstead, part of it dating from before the end of the 15th century, but with a later Georgian façade.

Further Information

Park Road, Banstead SM7 3AJ.

Park Road runs south from the Banstead War Memorial at the eastern end of Banstead High Street. The well is a short distance along Park Road on the left and cannot be missed.

On a public highway.

Image: Marion Woodward

The Sculpture Garden Ockley

The Hannah Peschar Sculpture Garden was the brainchild of Hannah Peschar and founded 36 years ago. It is based in the garden of a Grade II* 15th century cottage and was designed and planted by the award-winning landscape artist Anthony Paul.

Each year, from the beginning of April until the end of October, some 200 pieces of contemporary sculpture are exhibited within the garden grounds by around 50 UK and European artists in a wide range of materials and styles from the abstract to the more traditional - a dazzling artistic show within the beauty of the gardens.

Further Information

Black and White Cottage, Standon Lane, Ockley RH5 5QU.

From Ockley follow Standon Lane for about 0.8 miles. The entrance is marked by signs past a left turn to Okewood Church and before Gatton Manor Golf Course. Open: From April to end October. See the web site for actual dates and entrance costs.

www.hannahpescharsculpture.com

Image: Hannah Peschar Sculpture Garden

Betchworth Castle

A crumbling but interesting ruin overlooking the river Mole. Built as a castle in 1373 it was re-built as a fortified home in 1448. Later alterations were made in 1705 and again by Sir John Soane in 1799.

In 1834 Henry Thomas Hope added it to his Deepdene Estate, demolishing part of it for building materials. It gradually became a ruin and was looked on as a folly.

There was a fine avenue of lime trees leading up to it, now replaced by newer lime trees. Look to the left on the way up and you will see the only remnants of the original house, the elegant stables. Designed by Sir John Soane, these fine buildings, now houses, are patterned in Soane's 'primitive' style.

It is also worth crossing the road to the garden centre where, on the left as you enter, is a footpath leading from the carpark to Box Hill bridge, a fine Victorian iron structure.

Further Information

Reigate Road, Dorking RH4 1NZ (at Betchworth Golf Course).

Open at all times.

Images: Thomas Leitch

The Cranston Library

The Cranston Library is a small chamber over the vestry of St Mary Magdalene in Reigate. It was founded by the Reverend Andrew Cranston, Vicar of Reigate from 1697 to 1708; his motto and the date - 'Animi Alimentum : 1701' – are on the library door to this day.

Cranston's innovation was Reigate Publick Library; the books could be borrowed by the townspeople of Reigate and neighbourhood, making it a forerunner of public lending libraries in England. Adding to his own books through gifts and subscriptions, Cranston collected around 1,800 books by the time of his death in 1708. That year he established a Trust to protect the library, making the Vicar its Keeper; this trust secured the survival of the library, now in the care of nine trustees.

This is a rare example of a parish library surviving in situ, with a particularly rich collection of books dating mostly from the 17th and 18th centuries, and its history as an early lending library. Heritage Volunteers from The Arts Society Reigate care for the collection.

Further Information

St Mary's Church, Chart Lane, Reigate RH2 7RN.

Viewable by appointment only: cranstonlibrary@gmail.com

Full details: www.cranstonlibraryreigate.com

Image: Hilary Ely

Providence Chapel

This white weatherboard building, in Charlwood, with its wide veranda looks as if it might have been dropped into the Surrey countryside from the Southern States of America!

First built and used in Horsham in 1797 it was the guardhouse of barracks housing troops ready to repel a possible invasion by Napoleon Bonaparte's army.

After the battle of Waterloo in 1815 a Charlwood farmer bought the building and moved it from Horsham to Charlwood where it became a non-conformist chapel. It remained as a chapel until 2013 when dwindling congregations meant it closed and it was acquired by a trust who began to renovate the building and re-opened it in 2018.

Further Information

Providence Chapel, Chapel Road, Charlwood RH6 0DA.

Website: www.providencechapelcharlwood.org

Image: Michael Beach

Monumental Brasses

St Mary's Church, dating back to the late 7th century, is the oldest church in Surrey and one of the oldest in England. Amongst its many treasures are the two large memorial brasses in the floor of the beautiful Norman chancel which was built around 1240. The brasses commemorate Sir John d'Abernon II and Sir John d'Abernon III, the former believed to have died about 1325 and the latter between 1335 and 1350. The brass of the first Sir John is a magnificent life size image about six feet long and is unique in showing Sir John holding a lance as well as a sword. The workmanship, especially in the detailing of the chain mail is superb and the shield still possesses the original blue Limoges enamel. The lettering in the surrounding stone is part of a Norman French inscription.

The slightly smaller brass of Sir John III highlights the differences and changes in fashion of armour in the intervening years and the evolution of plate armour. This Sir John wears a chain mail shirt or hauberk over which he wears a solid armour breast plate and armour shin plates.

Both of the knights are standing on curious depictions of lions, which denote courage.

Further Information

St Mary's Church, Stoke Rd, Stoke d'Abernon KT11 3PX

The church is open between 2.00-4.00pm from April to October. Outside these hours please contact the Parish Administrator on 01932 866005.

www.stmarysstokedabernon.org.uk

Image: Michael Meurisse LRPS

Chatley Heath Semaphore Tower

The Grade II* listed Chatley Heath Semaphore Tower is the only surviving semaphore tower in Britain and stands deep in ancient heathland near Wisley in Surrey. This unique remnant from the Napoleonic era was once a vital link in a signalling chain that transmitted messages from Admiralty House in London to Portsmouth Docks in a matter of minutes. The construction of the line was ordered in 1816 in the aftermath of the Battle of Waterloo, when foreign invasion still seemed a real possibility. The Chatley Heath mast was the only station on the Portsmouth line that required a five-storey tower for visibility across the seven miles to its two neighbours and in 1822, on its completion, it was chosen to be the junction for another line to Plymouth. Thereafter, for over 20 years the urgent affairs of the Royal Navy passed back and forth along this line, relaying orders to the fleet and reporting the movements of friend and foe alike. With the coming of the railways the semaphore towers became less important and were decommissioned in 1847. The tower was used as a residence until the 1960s when it fell into disrepair. It has recently been refurbished by the Landmark Trust.

Further Information

Pointers Road, Wisley KT11 1PQ.

www.landmarktrust.org.uk

Image: Paul Fletcher

Chaldon Wall Painting

The Church of St Peter and St Paul at Chaldon dates back to Saxon times but most of what we see today is early medieval. Its chief glory is undoubtedly the mural painted on the west wall dating from the 12th century which is an attempt to illustrate the journey taken by souls after death to heaven or hell. In terms of its age and subject matter the painting is one of the most important in the country.

The work was limewashed over – probably during the Reformation – and only rediscovered in 1870 when the rector was in the throes of redecorating the interior. Since then, efforts have been made to restore and maintain the painting.

Measuring 17ft 3in by 11ft 2in, the Chaldon mural is a tempera painting using red and yellow pigments applied to dry plaster. The design is probably based on "The Ladder of Divine Ascent" written by John Climacus, a 6th-7th-century monk who lived in the monastery on Mount Sinai. It is divided into two horizontally, the upper half representing Purgatory and the lower half Hell. A ladder further subdivides the halves leading heavenwards towards the figure of Christ in a medallion. Many little figures scramble up the ladder in the hope of salvation. Some are gently helped on their way by angels but others tumble back into Hell where they join those already experiencing a variety of torments at the hands of large devils with prominent feet and gaping mouths.

Further Information

Church Lane, Chaldon CR3 5AL.

The church is normally open daily from 10am to 3pm.

www.chaldonchurch.co.uk

Images: Edward Howard

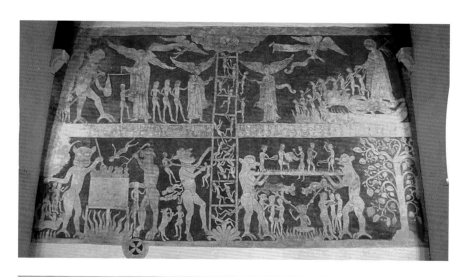

Dorking Museum & Heritage Centre

The museum explores the history of the town, its surrounding district and the lives of its many notable residents such as the composer Vaughan Williams. Displays feature geological and archaeological material and artefacts relating to local trade and transport, the area's great estates, tourism at Box Hill, the experience of the world wars, and the area's cultural contribution through its writers, artists, musicians, scientists and campaigners.

The museum houses a fine collection of local chalk fossils, including the skull of the rare Brachauchenius and the tail of a Mantellisaurus, as well as the mineral collection of Lord Ashcombe of Denbies. There are exhibits from the Bronze Age and Roman Dorking and local Saxon pottery. Other key items include a Wedgwood pottery collection, relating to the Wedgwood family's long association with the area, the Broadwood and Calvert costume collections, model racing cars celebrating the Dorking-based F1 Rob Walker Racing Team and a large collection of paintings, drawings and prints.

The photograph shows a penannular ring of the Late Bronze Age, c1150-750BC and was found in Betchworth. It is yellow gold with bands of paler sliver-rich gold. There is much debate about the purpose of these penannular rings. They are likely to have had a decorative function but it is not known for sure exactly how they were worn.

Further Information

The Old Foundry, 62 West Street, Dorking RH4 1BS.

www.dorkingmuseum.org.uk.

The Museum is open on Thursday, Friday and Saturday 10am to 4pm, and at other times for groups by appointment.

Image: Royston Williamson

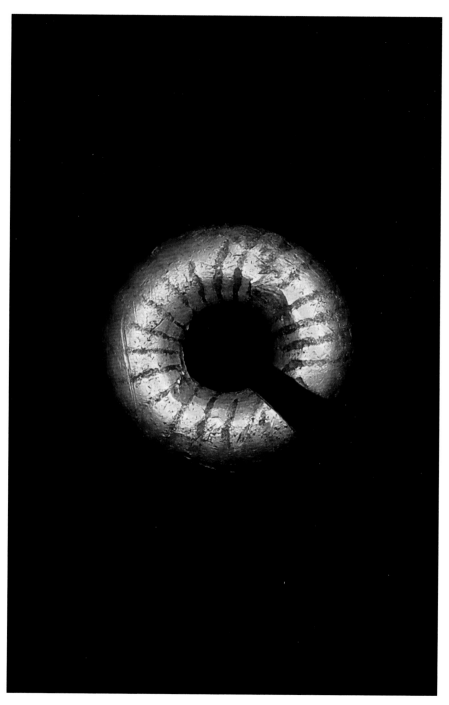

The Hope Mausoleum

Less than a mile from Dorking town centre, in Deepdene, lies the Hope Mausoleum. Erected in 1818, the mausoleum is a remarkable survivor of what was one of the most enigmatic of country estates, regarded as the locus classicus of Italian gardening from the 17th century. The estate featured one of the earliest Italian gardens and continued to be at the cutting edge of architectural design until the end of the 19th century. The mausoleum is the final resting place of the Regency arbiter of taste Thomas Hope and eight members of the Hope family including the 8th Duke of Newcastle, the last incumbent of Deepdene House. The Grade II* listed mausoleum, one of the earliest neo-Grecian buildings of its kind, was buried to roof level in the mid-20th century, which saw the breaking up of the estate and the demolition of the house and temple. It lay forgotten until recently when in 2016 (thanks to a £1 million Heritage Lottery Fund grant), the remnants of the Deepdene Estate were uncovered and restored to form The Deepdene Trail.

Further Information

Chart Park, Near Dorking Golf Club, Dorking RH5 4BX.

www.deepdenetrail.co.uk

Image: Alex Bagnall

Caterham Trio

Soper Hall. This fine building in the centre of the town is one of the last heritage buildings in Caterham. Built in 1911 in memory of William Soper (often referred to as the 'father of Caterham') it was originally the council offices and is now a community centre.

White Hill Tower. A folly, (in the grounds of Tower Farm but easily seen from the roadside) was built by Jeremiah Long, a local man, in 1862. Tradition has it that he built it in the hope that he could see the sea!

East Surrey Museum. This small attractive museum, housed in a Victorian flint and tiled building is dedicated to presenting the social history, archaeology and geology of East Surrey

(Soper Hall and the museum are within minutes of the railway station, a building that is also well worth a look!)

Further Information

Soper Hall, Harleston Valley Road, Caterham CR3 6HY.

East Surrey Museum, Stafford Road, Caterham CR3 6JG.
Normally open Wednesday, Thursday and Saturday.
www.eastsurreymuseum.org.uk

White Hill Tower, Stanstead Road, Caterham CR3 6 AS.

Images: Thomas Leitch

Leith Hill Tower

Leith Hill Tower surmounts the highest point in the Surrey Hills and indeed the SE of England with impressive views to the North as well as over the Weald. It was built in 1765 by Richard Hull of Leith Hill Place which is situated on the slopes to the south. At a time when the world was waking up to the beauties of the natural landscape Hull constructed the tower not as a residence or for any military purpose but so 'that you might obtain an extensive prospect over a beautiful country.' By the middle of the next century the building had fallen into disrepair and been sealed up but in 1864 the then owner William John Evelyn of Wotton (see Wotton House) reopened it, adding a new spiral staircase in its own adjoining turret built in a similar style. The construction is of Bargate Stone, a tough sandstone quarried at numerous sites along the Greensand Ridge in Surrey. The stone may even have been sourced in the immediate surroundings of the tower where there are signs of excavation. There are dressings and string courses of red brick.

The tower was acquired by the National Trust in 1923.

Further Information

Leith Hill, Dorking RH5 6LY.

www.nationaltrust.org.uk

Image: Arnhel de Serra

Lovelace Bridges

The 1st Earl of Lovelace, owner of the East Horsley Estate in the 19th Century, was an enthusiastic forester. In order to ease the transport of timber by horse drawn carts across the wooded hills to the south of his mansion Horsley Towers and avoid precipitous ascents and descents, he constructed tracks with gentle inclines and embankments. Bridges were built where his new tracks crossed existing bridleways or roads. The bridges were usually horseshoe shaped, and there were fifteen in all, of which ten remain. In size they range from the Dorking Arch with an impressive 18 ft span to the narrow Meadow Plat Bridge which is less than half that. The style of the bridges is surprisingly ornate, with a distinctive red brick and flint structure also to be seen in other buildings in the area, not least the Towers themselves. Bricks and mortar are likely to have been locally produced. (for example at Betchworth) All originally carried tile name plaques, but only two of these survive. The remaining bridges are Hermitage, Troye, Raven Arch, Briary Hill East, Briary Hill West, Robin Hood, Stony Dene, Oldlands, Meadow Plat and Dorking Arch.

Further Information

There is a Lovelace Bridges Trail produced by the Horsley Countryside Preservation Society.

www.hcps.online

Image: Paul Fletcher

Wotton House

The Evelyn family acquired the Wotton estate in 1579 and have been a presence there until our own times. The house was enlarged and modified many times over the centuries and much of what you see today dates back to the 19th and is the work of Henry Woodyer who restored the building after a fire in 1877. John Evelyn, scholar, diarist and friend of Pepys lived here in the last few years of his life after the death of his brother in 1699. Evelyn knew almost everyone who was anyone in the 17th century but although his famous diary provides an extensive commentary on political matters and spares the reader few details of the church services he attended, it says little about the house and gardens. However, we know that the latter were laid out by John Evelyn and a cousin in the middle of the 17th century and thought to be the first attempt to build an Italian garden in Britain ('amenitys not frequent in the best Noble mens Gardens in England' as he puts it.) A Doric temple faces the house on an artificial hill with terraces. There are also water features, statues and grottoes dating from the same period.

The house itself is now a hotel.

Further Information

Guildford Road Dorking RH5 6HS.

www.wottonhouse.co.uk

Image: Paul Fletcher

Betchworth Lime Quarries

The dramatic brick buildings rising out of the beautiful Surrey Wildlife Trust nature reserve are a spectacular reminder of the Surrey Hills industrial past, for this is also the site of the Betchworth/Brockham Lime Works.

This quarry and the one further towards Brockham grew up at the beginning of the 19th century taking the chalk from the hills above and converting it to lime in the kilns. There was a wide area of industrial activity including a small gauge railway track, buildings, kilns etc. all dedicated to the manufacture of lime. The work ceased in 1936, but traces of the kilns and buildings are still here and are scheduled as an ancient monument. A restoration project is in hand and the Surrey Wildlife Trust publishes a self-guiding trail to help you understand the site and its industrial history.

Further Information

The Coombe, Betchworth RH3 7BU.

Access is by foot via the North Downs Way or via The Coombe (just above Betchworth station) The nature reserve is always open, guided visits to the Lime Works may be available from time to time. Check the web site.

www.surreywildlifetrust.org/nature-reserves/betchworth-quarry-lime-kilns

Image: Thomas Leitch

The Cobhams of Lingfield

The church of St Peter & St Paul in Lingfield is the only Perpendicular church in Surrey and is notable for its double nave, its range of late medieval fittings and what Pevsner describes as the best set of brasses in the county. Although dating back to Saxon times, it is mostly 15th century and the work of Sir Reginald Cobham of Starborough Castle who also had an intercessionary college of priests built nearby in 1431.

Sir Reginald, who may well have fought at Agincourt, died 15 years later and is commemorated along with his second wife Anne in a prominent position in the chancel where they solemnly await the Day of Judgment. The tomb is of firestone with alabaster effigies. That of Sir Reginald is in the armour befitting a knight and his head rests on a helmet decorated with a Saracen's head. Beneath his feet reclines a lion. At his side his wife wearing widow's attire is attended by angels. Her feet rest on a wyvern.

A similar table monument commemorating an earlier Lord Cobham is situated in the North Chancel Chapel. Sir Reginald 1st Lord Cobham was a close associate of King Edward III and enjoyed a distinguished military career. His less refined effigy shows him in red, black and gilt painted armour of the day with his head likewise resting on a Saracen helmet. The other Saracen who supports his feet looks more than a little put out to have been allotted that particular role in perpetuity.

Further Information

Old Town Lingfield RH7 6AH.

www.lingfieldparishchurch.org

Images: Jill Harris

The Mill Church

Sitting on the highest point of Reigate Heath overlooking the golf course, the Reigate Heath post mill is a distinctive landmark for miles around. To the casual observer there is nothing to suggest that the robust-looking brick base of the building contains not the paraphernalia of a working mill but a church. The mill itself was probably erected around 1753 and until about 1870 wheat was taken from the Reigate downland to the mill to be ground. In 1880, however, the round base of the mill was converted into a chapel of ease to St Mary's, and named St Cross Chapel. The first service took place on 14 September 1880. It is reported that Sunday services were so well attended that 'as many people were outside as in.'

In 1900 Reigate Heath Golf Club purchased land containing the mill, which was then leased to St Mary's Church, with the club maintaining the structure. In 1962 the Borough Council bought the mill but continued the arrangement with St Mary's.

A survey at about this time revealed many weaknesses in the building's structure. In 1962-4 extensive remedial work was carried out and new sails were fitted. In 2000 there was a further major overhaul including once again the fitting of new sails. During this time a considerable proportion of the mill's machinery remained in place.

The Mill Church now holds services on one Sunday each month in the summer. There is also a carol service before Christmas as well as occasional services by arrangement.

Further Information

Flanchford Road Reigate RH2 8AB.

Image: Ian Capper

Regiment of Trees

In open land not far from the Epsom racecourse lies Langley Vale Wood, one of four woods commissioned by the Woodland Trust as part of their First World War centenary project (2014–18). It is the Trust's flagship First World War centenary site and the largest of these woods, extending over 640 acres. Parts of the site are ancient woodland and farming also went on here over many centuries. During the First World War, the Walton and Tadworth end of the site was used for army training and there were trenches, a rifle range, a gas training school and a camp. In our own time, over 100,000 trees have been planted here to create new woodlands and in one location 80 trees have been planted in a grid formation with stone soldiers taking the place of some of the trees. The Regiment of Trees was created with sculptor Patrick Walls to commemorate the day in January 1915 that Lord Kitchener came to Epsom Downs to inspect 20,000 troops, all volunteers from the 2nd London Division of Kitchener's New Army. It had snowed overnight and the recruits had risen at 4am in order to be in their places in good time for the great man's arrival although some of them were not even fully kitted out. In the event Kitchener didn't arrive until much later that morning by which time there had been several injuries and cases of hypothermia. The twelve life-sized soldiers who commemorate the event were carved by Patrick Walls from Hill House Edge sandstone and stand among a mix of native broadleaf trees.

Further Information

Langley Vale Wood, Headley Road, Ashtead, Epsom, KT18 6BB.

www.woodlandtrust.org.uk/visiting-woods/woods/langley-vale-wood

Image: Mike Longhurst FRPS

Leith Hill Musical Festival

The title of this Festival represents the highest summit in this area of Surrey and the Festival motto "Music won the Cause" was chosen by the original committee. The idea for the Festival was sown in 1904 by two ladies, Evangeline Farrer and Margaret Vaughan Williams, sister of Ralph Vaughan Williams conductor and composer whose statue stands outside the Dorking Halls. A committee of twelve volunteers asked local choirs if the singers would be interested in taking part in a competition and an opportunity to sing together in a grand concert. The first Festival took place in 1905 with seven choirs. Within ten years the Festival had sixteen choirs taking part. Since then nearly fifty choirs have at some time or other joined in this opportunity to sing with others. In 1921 a 'Children's Choirs day' was added to the Festival. The conductor at the Festival until 1953 was Ralph Vaughan Williams. He has been followed by just five further conductors. Nowadays the morning competitions include short pieces for all singers, and smaller groups. The afternoon is spent rehearsing with an orchestra and the evening concert is open to the public. The children's day continues and other musical events are often included during each year.

Further Information

Concerts are held annually in Dorking.

www.lhmf.org.uk

Images: Thomas Leitch/Leith Hill Music Festival

Lingfield Cross and Cage

The Cross and Cage in Lingfield together have the appearance of a tiny church but were constructed separately. St Peter's Cross is thought to have been constructed in the 15th century by the Cobham family (See separate entry.) It marked the boundary between two parishes at the time. The cross itself may have been removed by puritanical folk – iconoclasts – in the centuries that followed. A flat plinth now surmounts the pyramidal roof of Horsham slabs. The 'Cage' which abuts the Cross was erected much later in 1773. It is actually a cell built of stone in which local wrongdoers could be locked up and was last used as such in 1882 when a poacher was temporarily incarcerated there.

Adjacent to Cross and Cage stands the Lingfield Oak – now completely hollow with a girth of 6.94m and thought to be over 400 years old – a genuinely ancient tree.

Further Information

Old Town Lingfield RH7 6AH.

www.historicengland.org.uk/listing/the-list/list-entry/1205403

Image: Jill Harris

West Horsley Place

West Horsley Place is a Grade I listed manor house dating from the 15th century. With remarkably surviving interiors from the 16th to the 18th century and with little 19th or 20th century intervention, West Horsley Place displays the evolution of country house architecture during this period.

The house has passed through the hands of illustrious owners, including Henry VIII – who enjoyed a 35-course lunch in the Stone Hall - Carew Raleigh, son of Sir Walter Raleigh, and Lady Elizabeth Fitzgerald, 'Fair Geraldine' of the Earl of Surrey's famous sonnet. Queen Elizabeth I is known to have stayed on several occasions. More recently, in 2014 historian and former presenter of University Challenge, Bamber Gascoigne, unexpectedly inherited West Horsley Place from his aunt, Mary, Duchess of Roxburghe. Decades of benign neglect had taken their toll on the house and also on the eight Grade II listed structures situated on the estate. In October 2016, West Horsley Place was placed on the Historic England 'Heritage at Risk' register. To conserve and repair the house, outbuildings and estate, and to give them a new life and purpose, Bamber and Christina Gascoigne have generously transferred ownership of West Horsley Place to a charity, the West Horsley Place Trust (formerly the Mary Roxburghe Trust). The Trust is seeking to establish at West Horsley Place a welcoming space for the community to share and enjoy with arts, culture, community, history and nature at its heart.

Further Information

Epsom Road Leatherhead KT24 6AN.

www.westhorsleyplace.org

Images: Richard Lewisohn

Church of the Wisdom of God

At the end of a rather unremarkable road in Lower Kingswood is a very remarkable little church. The church of the Wisdom of God is unique in England: it is built like a Roman basilica and is filled with treasures from ancient Rome and Byzantium. The church was the inspiration of two Victorians, Dr Edwin Freshfield and Sir Cosmo Bonsor, both with an interest in archaeology and both residents of Kingswood. The church was designed by the architect Sidney Barnsley in accordance with their wishes. It was built by the local firm of Murray and was dedicated on the 17th July, 1892.

Outside, the impression is of a small squat, pink building huddled in trees, the pinkness deriving from a mixture of brick and stone, some of the brick being used decoratively in Byzantine lattice and herringbone patterns. Like a Roman basilica, the church is rectangular and the view inside is dominated by a striking central apse on the eastern, altar wall. This is coated with a variety of marbles and a mosaic of gold leaf in the manner of Roman and Byzantine basilicas. Most of the marbles are Roman: some come from Roman columns and others from blocks left in ancient quarries in the Middle East. The exceptions are the newer marbles on the floor of the nave and chancel and some of the marbles in the baptistery. The aisles have fragments of 5th/6th century Byzantine capitals. The wooden 'wagon' roof and church furniture are by Barnsley himself. A short distance from the church stands a curious weatherboarded campanile with a lead-covered dome based on a tower Freshfield had seen in Bulgaria.

Further Information

Buckland Road, Lower Kingswood KT20 7DN.

www.parishofkingswood.org.uk

Image: Parish of Kingswood/Alexia Hartman.

Ewell and Holman Hunt

Hunt commenced his famous painting 'The Light of the World', illustrating Revelations 3.20, in an orchard in Worcester Park Farm. Then, on a path by the Hogsmill River, Hunt found an abandoned hut once used by gunpowder workers. The overgrown door of the hut appears in the painting as does a specially commissioned lantern. Hunt worked by night to get the effect of the moonlight "in a little sentry-box, built of hurdles, with his feet in a sack of straw".

The original painting now hangs in Keble College, Oxford, but a copy can be seen nearby at St Mary the Virgin Ewell Parish Church. This copy was the sole survivor of a devastating fire in the north aisle of the church in November 1973.

In 1847, Hunt painted the largely 13th century original church, demolished shortly afterwards. Sir George Glyn, vicar, seeing the artist busy in the churchyard, offered to buy the picture if it was done well. The original painting is owned by Baron Lloyd Webber, but a copy hangs in St Mary's. Holman Hunt knew Ewell well and in 1847 was staying with his aunt and uncle, who lived at Rectory Farm in Church Street, Ewell.

Further Information

St Mary the Virgin Ewell Parish Church, London Road, Ewell, KT17 2AY.

www.stmarysewell.com

Images: Nishi Sharma

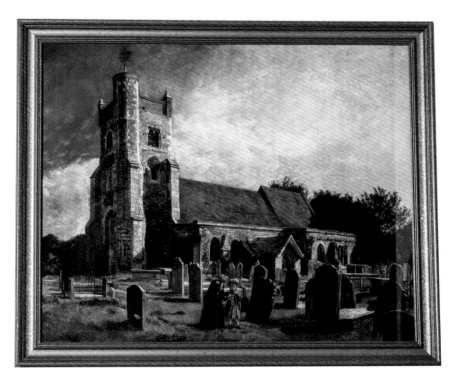

'THE LIGHT OF THE WORLD'
Side window for the burnt-out North side. His reproduction of
Holman Hunt's famous painting was salvaged after the
disastrous fire of 20.11.11. The upper half of the frame was
badly charred but burn marks can still be seen.

Grave Boards

In early times grave boards were commonly used to mark graves. These consisted of an oak board carrying an inscription and supported by oak posts at the head and foot ends of the grave. The widespread use of these grave markers, which were cheaper than stone, stopped in Victorian times and it is extremely rare for any to have survived. However, in the section on Mickleham in the 1971 version of The Buildings of England – Surrey by Nairn and Pevsner it is stated "Mickleham is almost the only Surrey churchyard to have taken the trouble to preserve its GRAVE-BOARDS, which it was a local habit to erect. There are three grave boards dated 1813, 1886 and 1887." The boards have been renovated.

In addition, there are two modern boards in Mickleham churchyard. One dated 1995 is a memorial to John Sankey, nationally known environmental educationalist. The other dated 2010 marks the place where the remains of 17 burials, discovered under the vestry floor during rebuilding, have been reinterred.

Further Information

St Michael and All Angels, Old London Road, Mickleham RH5 6DU.

Images: Ben Tatham

In Memory of Anne Maria Remnant

December 7th 1867   Aged 77 years old

In Memory of John Walker   who died

January 23rd 1813.

Aged 83 years

John Hart Peters Sankey
24 June 1917 – 7 April 1995

The Mystery Column

On Reigate Heath, often hidden by the trees and close to the A25, is an elegant cast iron Corinthian column. It has clearly been there for many years and it looks like a Victorian artefact. But what is it for, why is here and who erected it? It is on the site of a race course that was in this area between 1835 and 1864, so it is possibly a remaining relic of the course.It has also been suggested that it is a stink pipe But it is an unusual and elegant sight in the beauty of Reigate Heath.

Also of interest is the Heath Church on Flanchford Road. Entering from the A25 and beyond the row of houses on the left, the tin built church (sister church of St Mary's) is a build-it-yourself Victorian chapel that started life as a Congregational church at Shaws Corner, Redhill.

Further Information

From the A25 drive into Flanchford Road and park in the car park facing the heath. Walk forward to the trees ahead and follow the footpath sign on the right, after about 500 metres the column is on the left.

Always open (for Church openings see church notice boards and the church web site).

Image: Thomas Leitch

The Running Horse

One of the oldest buildings in Leatherhead, The Running Horse on the bank of the River Mole dates back to 1403. It was built on land that belonged to the church and was originally known as Rumminges House after Eleynor Rumminge who was written about in a poem by John Sketton, Henry VIII's poet. The poem can still be found on a wall in the pub. Legend says that Elizabeth I spent a night at the inn due to the flooding of the River Mole. Alongside the inn is the beautiful Leatherhead Bridge with its 14 elegant arches. The bridge was rebuilt in 1783 and is a favourite of many artists. It stands on medieval piers.

Further Information

38 Bridge Street, Leatherhead KT22 8BZ.

Image: June Robinson

Emily Davison in Epsom

Emily Wilding Davison died in Epsom hospital three days after falling under the King's horse during the 1913 Derby. Her death was one of the most shocking episodes in the suffragettes' campaign to win the vote for women. Emily was courageous, extremely clever, hardworking and well liked.

Since January 2018 the Emily Davison Memorial Project committee have been fundraising and commissioned sculptor, Christine Charlesworth, to create a life-size portrait figure. Christine wanted the sculpture to be natural and approachable. Emily sits on a pale granite bench, turned to whoever is beside her as though in deep, animated conversation. Emily had two university degrees and loved reading, so, beside her are three of her favourite books and the mortar board she always wore on Suffragette marches. Emily is wearing the hat she wore at the Derby and also has all her medals and badges on her jacket. She is holding a census form. There is a short video available to listen to as people sit beside Emily giving many details of her life and items depicted in the sculpture.

The sculpture is due to be unveiled in early June 2021 and will sit in Epsom Market Square close to the clock tower.

Further Information

Epsom Clock Tower, Epsom KT19 8BA.

Image and details: Christine Charlesworth MRSS SWA.

**THE ARTS
SOCIETY**
EAST SURREY
AREA

ARTS SOCIETIES IN EAST SURREY

We hope that reading this book will encourage you to join one of our Societies, and enjoy the interest and inspiration that comes from our talks, visits and holidays. Do check the websites of any of the societies below to find out what's on and who to contact.

THE ARTS SOCIETY, EAST SURREY AREA COMMITTEE

ASHTEAD	tas-ashtead.org.uk
BETCHWORTH	theartssocietybetchworth.org.uk
BOOKHAM	theartssocietybookham.org.uk
CHEAM	theartssocietycheam.org.uk
CHIPSTEAD	theartssocietychipstead.org.uk
CLAREMONT	claremontartssociety.org.uk
COBHAM & OXSHOTT	artssocietycobhamandoxshott.org.uk
DORKING	theartssocietydorking.org.uk
EPSOM	theartssocietyepsom.org.uk
HORSLEY	theartssocietyhorsley.org.uk
HORSLEY LOVELACE	theartssocietyhorsleylovelace.org.uk
LEATHERHEAD	theartssocietyleatherhead.org.uk
LIMPSFIELD	theartssocietylimpsfield.org.uk
REIGATE	theartssocietyreigate.org.uk
WALTON ON THE HILL	theartssocietywaltononthehill.org.uk

**THE ARTS
SOCIETY**
EAST SURREY
AREA

ACKNOWLEDGEMENTS

Our thanks to those members of The Arts Society who have made contribution to the book.

Marion Woodward

June Robinson

Barbara Lyner

Alan Clarke

Hilary Ely

Derek Kay

Sue Tatham

Thanks also to Thomas Leitch for various photographs.

**THE ARTS
SOCIETY**
EAST SURREY
AREA

FIFTY TREASURES OF THE SURREY HILLS

INDEX